Bits & Pieces

After Therapy for Black Women

Also by Ebony Payne-English

The Random Happenings
Secrets of Ma'at

Bits & Pieces

After Therapy for Black Women

Ebony Payne-English

NEW Reads Publications | Jacksonville

Published in the United States by NEW Reads Publications. NEW Reads Publications is a registered trademark of NEW Reads Publications, LLC in Jacksonville, FL.

newreadspub.com

Library of Congress Cataloging-in-Publication Data is available upon request.

ISBN 978-1-7357219-4-1 (hardback)
ISBN 978-1-7357219-5-8 (ebook)

Printed in the United States of America

Interior design by Nikesha Elise Williams
Cover design by Nicole "Nico" Holderbaum

First Edition: July 2022

*For my Mable, Mattie, Joyce Ann, Brenda,
Regina, Renica, Sherica, Stephanie, Tamera,
Akemi, Miracle, Na'Kima, Shaleka, Jasmine,
and all the colored girls who've considered
suicide when the rainbow is enough.*

Contents

Bits & Pieces IV: Fact Check

Bits & Pieces V: Commitment Issues

Bits & Pieces VI: PMS

Bits & PIeces *I*
Menstruation

My relationship with my period starts with a curse. A curse that belonged to the first woman for feeding her husband a piece of fruit that God put there in the first place; for some serpent that God created in the first place to tell her to eat. When she did, her husband, who was the one God told not to eat it in the first place, wanted some. So, she gave it to him and now I have a period.

I used to ask God to turn me into a gift for my husband. I wanted to disassociate my femininity from the fall of man so I treated my love life like a hero's quest. My mission: to save the men I loved from themselves. My period quickly became my kryptonite. When it came, my partner disappeared for three to five days at a time. If I mentioned the word tampon, he'd cringe.

A Caribbean man once told me he could not eat my cooking while I was on my period because during that time, a woman is "unclean." I shrugged my shoulders, told him more for me, and finished my plate. But for the longest time, I hated the monthly emotional whirlwind menstruation instigated in my life.

A few Biology classes and a childbirth later, for the first time, I finally get it. My cycle is my body's way of cleansing itself. It's a renewal. Sometimes, cleansing requires more than a physical purge. There is so much that we as Black women mush and suppress into our deepest most secret places just to get by, day to day, without having a nervous breakdown.

For five to seven days of every month my body gives me permission to cry. And for 22 years, had duped me into believing that it was for no reason at all. The whole time, it was to keep me from imploding from the pressure of my own unspoken trauma.

The Wind Is My Mother

The wind is my mother.
The air bends to her will
The trees curtsy at the sight of her regalia
The sand, storms her feet and offers security

She carries ocean on her breeze
She blows in a direction I cannot follow at
times
Expanding herself wide and encompassing

I have witnessed first hand her power
Seen her anger topple a tower
Her globetrotting gusts are the origin of my
wanderlust
Great minds of old have yet to grasp the gist of
her existence

I listen to her churn outside my window
I never learned to whistle
I have always been inherently clumsy
I was not gifted her gracefulness

Ebony Payne-English 15

I was, contrarily, granted her propensity to
carry things

I bury things inside of me deep
It often impedes my sleep
When I weep, the wind chimes outside my
home
Reminding me that I am never alone

How I long to be as massive as my mother
How small I feel when she tsunamis my name
"We are the same," she tells me.

I do not gain the confidence she aims to instill
with that statement
She flurries me with patience
Greatness requires gestation
The wind does not speak in layman's
Too afraid she may lose me in translation.

Love In 4 Parts

I.

   Says Meg Thee Stallion to the teenager,
"You don't send your own nudes. Fuck these
tricks! They don't deserve to see your real
titties."
   Says the teenager to Meg, "You're a
genius!"

I lost my virginity to the love of my life inside of
a trap house
I was seventeen years young, dumb, and
dangerous
But only to myself

I had never felt more of a rush
Than the first time he touched me beautiful
Than that one time he kissed me confident
When he danced me desirable and sexed me
worthy
I needed the validity.

Teenage girls be needing that sometimes.
It is often paid for with pain
It cost him not a thing to pay me no mind

When he went off to find something new
I changed my hue that day

II.

        Says Ari Lennox to the sixth grader,
"Don't date these niggas till you're 43."
        Says the fifth grader to Ari, "I hadn't
planned on it."

I made-out with the love of my life for the first
time
When I was 12 years insecure
The skinny, nerdy, awkward, bookworm
Who liked Tupac Shakur, X-Men, and climbing
trees
Couldn't believe a popular boy had a crush on
me

He tongued me down on a park bench and I
burst into blush
Kept that color up until he changed
Pink is still my favorite color
Just a different shade

III.

Says Sarafina Ethereal to the college
student, "I don't chase 'em, I replace 'em."
Says the college student to Fina, "I feel
you."

I conceived a child with the love of my life the
summer after my freshman year of undergrad
The girl he was cheating on me with was big
mad
And tried to jump me at a funeral
I had an abortion the next day and we never
spoke again
I don't think of him often
Or the seven years of my formative period I
spent loving him
With an underdeveloped heart and a teenaged
brain

I refrain from painting myself the victim
Instead I collect checks
From the lessons I get off the tricks men play
Games are only fun if there's a possibility of
victory
You are deserving of reciprocity

IV.

    Says Che to the 35 year old me, "Just being an honest woman does good for us who feel deeply."
    Says me to the homie, "My honesty has saved me a thousand times over."

And sometimes honest looks like
Biiiiiiiiiiiiiiitch!!!!!!
One minute we were talking love languages
And the next we were having sex
And it was great . . . and I'm ok

Fragile

I have never loved a man
                          who planted his feet
Well enough to hold me up
                          when I lean in.

Although a gentle giant,
The rough and uncomfortable truth is
Gentleness
Does not mask the weight of my grandeur
To gentlemen callers trying to collar a bad bitch
Only to end up with an open mouthed goddess
on the other end of their line

By the time they decide to cast me back to the
sea
For a fish more comparable to the plenty
I've already proven too massive to fling
And too loyal to unhook

I have been dragged behind the boat, mistook
for Moby Dick
Piranha-ish male energy plagues my intimacy
Me be conquest
Presumed conquered by casual lovers
Who hover their conjugal gaze over me
unarmored

Ebony Payne-English 21

Still un-garnered by those who half court a
woman with a full support system

My catch and release game is devoid of drama
I am calmed by karma
I can wish you well on your way to hell
With a smile on my face and a warm embrace
I don't take frailty personally
I take accountability for being a lot.
The cost to be with a boss
Is proportionate to the gift that you got

What I gave away was too much for what was
required of them.
I reset and raised my standards
Never again will I be enamored by beautiful
words
Forever moved by momentous actions
And displayed compassion for the tasking
Of offering your whole and healed heart
Still full of surgical scars——

To another . . .

Bits & PIeces *II*
Departure
Cleansing

So, here I am. Day two of my first period of 2019; sobbing at my desk and jabbing into my keyboard a very unpopular opinion and for me, the most uncomfortable truth: Superman is a deadbeat dad.

I remember watching *Superman Returns*. I remember the underwhelming feeling it left me with. But what I remember most is watching Superman, upon learning he had fathered a child with Lois Lane, leave the planet! Not the city. Not the country. HE. LEFT. EARTH!

I remember being the only one of my nerdy, comic book head ass friends to be upset, disturbed, and wildly offended. At the time, I didn't get why it bothered me so much. I just knew it did.

2 Part Question

We all know the man can fuck
But can he love?
Yes.
But can he love me?
No!

Never stopped him from trying though
Even after I lay crying in those arms of his
Writhing over the fragments of the heart he'd
just torn into
He vowed to love me through it
And I can admit that he tried.

He tried so hard to make love
Only to just end up fucking me over and over
Both orgasm and betrayal
Birthed new lies that tasted true on the tip of
my tongue
I swore never to leave his side while he was
deep inside
I swore never to call again each time he sinned
With every contradiction, I trusted myself less

I've lost all respect for romance
And chemistry
Passion pottered me an empty vessel

Insecure and unsure
Jealous and wildly aggressive
It has been said that whores cause confusion

Who would've thought I'd give my all to a
t.h.o.t.
That would make such nothing of my sacred
spaces

I took him to Miami once
Told him it was the happiest place I ever lived
Told him I've never been taken by a man on
vacation
Told him if he was interested in staying, we
could move

He eclipsed that mood with a heartfelt
confession
Of yet another indiscretion
I tell myself out loud that I am not crazy
I forgive myself at night when I stalk his page
I FaceTime Black women
Who offer no judgment for the fool I've
manifested out of myself

They tell me they've all been there
They tell me even despair looks beautiful on me
There is no need for me to attempt to smile
They see right past my magic

We straight face mourn the tragic loss of the
soft places

Growing harder inside of me before our very
eyes
Vulnerability has never been kind to somebody
like me

Chunks & Pits

The life of the party died several deaths
Prior to putting on her red lipstick
And arriving at your shindig
She got evicted yesterday

It has been three days since her last full meal
She awaits the bus in six-inch heels
Wearing earbuds
Singing of love, sex, and chicken wings

The life of the party really hates the radio
She dances alone in the middle of the floor
Until her feet are sore
Until she is sweaty and sticky and dizzy
Until she feels alive again

She's had several resurrections this year
One day she will choose not to resuscitate
But that day is not today

The DJ is playing all her favorite songs
The life of the party hates to go home
Not until it is done
And all the liquor is drunk
And all the herb is in plumes
She has packed her whole life
Into one spinning room after another

At her brother's house
Whenever she goes out,
He tells her to grow up

The life of the party feels stuck
Somewhere between beauty queen
And starving artist
She is a very guarded and complex soul

No one quite knows how she ticks
No one quite knows how to fix her
She spins round the full circle
Center of attention

A syncopated broken beautiful
She smiles
Her usual come hither horizon of a smirk
The life of the party is a flirt
One disaster away from a trainwreck

She reflects during long car rides
Confides in her Uber drivers
Smears her makeup on a stranger's chest
Every now and again
When she feels the need to be close
To something . . . breathing

Desocialized

I miss the stages
The creaky ones
The small ones
The shiny wood platforms
The ones covered in marley
The ones with Garvey flags
The ones that have DJ booths

And I miss the DJs too
The ones who master groove
The soulful dudes
The hip hop heads
The club goes crazy ladies
The curators of the culture
The local ones
The global phenoms
The ones whose spins aren't for sale

And I miss the clubs as well
The crowded kind
The ones with no line
The dancehalls
The ones with fog
The ones with poetry
The ones who let women in free
The ones where men don't harass me
The ones with strippers

The ones with the food truck that sells
honeydrippers at 2 A.M.

Y'all, I miss them
By them I meant my tribe
The ones with the vibe
The ones made of light
The ones who can still feel bright in a room full
of stars
The ones who stay charged

The ones who always pay you back
The ones who watch your back
The ones who never front
The ones who can be blunt without being
disrespectful
The ones who are careful in their dealings
The ones who offer safety to express your
feelings and truths
I love you
I love you
I do

Before COVID19 ravaged small businesses in
this country,
Jacksonville's elbow broke
Our favorite bars closed
Our black owned cigar lounge got bought out
Shad Khan's northern connects moved to the
south
The price of rent went through the roof
Forcing so many local owners into retirement
And now downtown is shiny with diamanté

And I miss Thursdays
The Ill Clinton kind
The Black on Black Rhyme nights
The Cypher hosted by Love Reigns
The ones that came with chaining ceremonies
The ones that weren't this lonely

Bits & PIeces *III*
Birth Story

It was Halloween of 2013. I was getting ready for a show. A phone call came. It was a stranger on the other end saying he was new to the area and a mutual friend had given him my contact information. He was looking for the poetry spots. I invited him to the show that night and ended the conversation.

He showed up and in full Disney princess fashion, I fell in love at first sight of this beautiful superhero of a man who came and slayed all my demons and dragons in one night. He was also kind enough to give me the dick down of the millennium along the way. Four years later, we conceived our first child together.

Are You There Love?

Misery means to be my muse
I have a new tattoo
It is placed just above my left breast
It is beneath flesh
It is lightning bolt scar through the center of
my heart
I am healing.

You have bloomed into the most beautiful bud
I've ever had
The most friendly lover leaves thorn prints in
my skin
When I squeeze too tightly
When I release too wildly
When I don't know how to hold you close

Closed palm is too close to keep
I fear that we've drifted too deep to breathe
I am unrested during our reprieves
Although I'm safer when alone
I find myself at home curled fetal
Into the tucked cuddle of your arms
And I want to belong there

I long to feed from the fruit of this labor
Instead I am starving for attention . . . mostly
to detail

I know quite well how we do
But what we are doing is a mystery

You have taught me in exemplary fashion about
acceptance
I feel tested on my cognition of the
unacceptable
I would love to flow freely
Like ivy streaming green chakra shockwaves
Over, under, and through anything that
separates you

Are you here love?
Will you stay love?
Are you afraid love?
Me too.

Meditation I: Be Still

Dear Mahogany Rose:

The forest that named you is ablaze
Your mother is a burning bush
Orating sacred wisdom to wise young writers of
words

On April 11, 2017 I took a pregnancy test in a
Baltimore restaurant bathroom
Your Aunt Ama waited outside the stall
I had just wrapped *On Purpose* the night before
That was the first thing we ever performed
together

During the time I was pregnant with you, it was
difficult for me to write
I wanted so badly to finish my novels, tour my
play, and continue teaching

You required me to take a moment
Be still.

If I am not writing
If I am not performing
If I am not traveling or teaching or helping or
giving or speaking or dancing . . .

Ebony Payne-English 40

If I am simply resting and breathing, it is
because you taught me that I be . . .
Still.

I am defined first by my relationship to self and
I needed a timeout.

Family Tree

If I were a tree
I would be a family
Unbroken
Straight spined

Where I'm from,
Strange fruit don't bloom off the vine often
It just hangs on dead to would be olive
branches
Extending from the soiled soul of southern
bigotry
And good Christian people

When I bloom,
I want it to be loud
I want it to be a thunderous occurrence
Like the sonic boom fragrance of fresh
magnolias

My leaves grow brilliant on my family tree
My trunk, the strongest Ebony
Carries the weight of a pain
That gave birth to a thornless Rose
Who will never know the concrete block
That crack had drawn between her mother and
kinfolk

Ebony Payne-English 42

Mahogany will know her people to be the
brightest defiance
Of Alabama mud bound
Florida stand your ground
Pitiful propaganda politics

My roots trace back to a farm raised grandpa
Moving his sweetheart who would later become
my grandma
To Chicago on a prayer and a promise that is
still kept

Over 62 years later
The way my hair flows like Spanish moss
Dancing in the wind
You would've thought it could sense
That I am a seed of grandpa's promise
Still reaching to manifest its fruit

And when it blooms
It will be just as sweet as granny
Just as ripe as mama's smile
Just as wild as it is fresh
Yes
It will be glorious

Bits & PIeces *IV*
Fact Check

Here are the facts.

Up until becoming pregnant with his child, I had always known my daughter's father to be giving, patient, understanding, and diligent. He was attentive to my needs, he listened when I spoke, and was an excellent provider.

When I became pregnant, things went south for my partner financially. He took a major loss one quarter and his company folded. After that, the man I knew became a ghost and has not yet returned.

I had an extremely high-risk pregnancy. He missed every doctor's appointment. He showed up the morning of my emergency Cesarean and left four days later, our daughter still in the NICU after being born prematurely. She was there for eight weeks. I never missed a day. He never visited once.

I brought her home from the hospital in an Uber. She is 4 years old now and I am still wondering where Superman ran off to. For several years, there was a man in my life who said all the right things, did all the right things, and treated me like the Queen I always knew I was. I had never been happier in my life than I was when I was with my daughter's father. Everyone saw the difference in me.

His absence is not only noticeable, it is an exclaiming elephant in the room at family gatherings, social events, and special occasions. When people ask about what happened, I can never seem to find the words. Furthermore, it's not really anybody's business. So I mush and suppress, and when my period comes . . .

. . . I cry.

Sink or Swim

I scream I'm drowning
You tell me how well you swim
You are not my friend
Nor are you my enemy
We are just two people
Who know things about each other

If only that knowledge was powerful enough to
foster love
Give it a good home
Raise it as if it were our own

Whenever I leave you alone
You act as if you haven't asked me to
I was good to you
That was bad for me
Your sweet talk rots my teeth
Fills my chest with cavities

I plug the holes with poems and children and
travel
I've no gavel
I'm no judge
I've just had enough

I cannot love me for the both of us
I attempted to gain the kind of rapport

In which your support does not catch me by
surprise
In which your attention
Is not disguised as ambivalence or rejection
I attempted to maintain the kind of connection
Where when you tell me you love me
What I'm thinking is, "I know."
Instead of, "I hope so."

When you tell me you're just going with the
flow,
I never understand what our current situation
might be
So I tread lightly and slow
But the undertow grabs hold of me
And I can no longer breathe life
Into this sunken relationship

A Song For Maya

Beloved say, life tried to choke the song from
her throat
That's why she sings with such passion

Now, here I am asking for a melody
Not knowing how in the hell that she survived
Her music stayed alive
But it did

Beloved say, with the kids in the house
Her husband tried to choke the song out her
mouth
That's why she sings with such passion

Now, here I am asking for a note
Not knowing how in the hell what she married
into
She was able to cope
But she did

Beloved say her song is a gift
Beloved say the caged bird sings
To remind herself of being a bird
To remind herself of wings and wind
And when she was free

Now here I am asking her to sing with me

Not knowing how in the hell we gone learn to
be birds again
But we breathe deep, open our beaks, and fly

Bitter

"Jealousy is just love and hate at the same time."

~Aubrey Graham

He told me he was jealous
I took it as a compliment

It entered my ears as a term of endearment
Felt protected and attractive

I handled his passive aggressive
With reassurance and excessive attention

I made myself too small to mention
Shrank into the depths of myself
To help him feel worthy of me
Deserving of my intimacy

Us Black girls really be magic!

We can love until we make ourselves disappear
I hadn't seen myself in years . . .

. . . Nobody even noticed I was missing

Bits & PIeces *V*
Commitment Issues

During my pregnancy, my daughter's father lost almost everything he worked so hard for including his sobriety from cocaine. That broke him. It dimmed him. Eventually, he withdrew to the other side of the country to rebuild his business, heal, plan, and get himself together. I respect that. I encourage as well as affirm his right and necessity to regroup, collect himself, and grow.

There's just one issue: OUR DAUGHTER, SIR!

Over the course of 22 months, I spent every dime of savings, maxed out my credit cards, and took out loans. I swallowed my pride and did things I never imagined I would do, asked favors from people I never thought I'd need; all because as a mother, failure is not an option.

I don't have the luxury of taking a year or two to collect myself after things fall apart. I have to dust myself off, dry my eyes, get up, and make breakfast. Then, pack her bag so I can get us out of the door in time to be on time for work.

There are days I want to be angry. I want to show up to his doorstep with the baby and just say, "I'm taking some time off. Figure it out!"

Anytime I think that, I immediately check myself. It is not my daughter's fault. I will not punish her and leave her on a stranger's doorstep simply because they share the same DNA and life is not fair.

When I hear people say things like, "Be careful who you have your kids by," I can't help but laugh at the irony.

I was in a loving and committed relationship. I was over 30 and gainfully employed, and he was over 30 and gainfully employed. We were happy and in what we thought to be a stable union. How could I have known that my Superman/Knight in Shining Armor/Prince Charming would take the lifeboat for himself and leave me and my daughter to kick it with the band while the ship went down?

Why am I so mad at myself even though I know I could not have known things would play out this way?

Why am I the one embarrassed that he is not in his child's life?

The answer is . . .

. . . I'm ashamed to be a single mother.

Creative Counseling

She tells me to focus more on the positive in
my life when I write
And ain't that how all Black girls were raised?

What goes on in this house, stays
That's how my body learned to carry the weight
Of arrayed trauma piercing the armor of my
solar plexus

Imbued upon my bruised psyche
Are the most unspeakable honesties
I censored my animosity for a spell
Eventually I had to tell the inaudible truths
That became a noose and strangled my glow

My body an abandoned home
Soulfulness forgone
Autopilot was on and effective

Perfected the smile and nod
Defrauded my memory bank
Feigned evergreen contentment
Took extended stays above the fray
In the age of fake it till you make it to a place
Preventing earnest enjoyment because it's
devoid

Of some form of therapy, healthy coping
mechanism, and relief

My poetry may not be as celebratory as you'd
hoped
But poems have been the antidote on many
occasions

When muted demons came ailing me suicidal
And denial beguiled me away from counseling
The prose in me still kept it real
Rhyme schemes helped me heal
Meter teetered on the edge of my sanity
When I was dangling from the ledge

In gratuity, I have pledged my pen
To give in to the voiceless pain we attempt to
restrain
So as not to ruin anyone's day with our baggage
I write to unpack it
And perhaps some day,
Find comfort in my most uncomfortable truths

Laugh Now, Cry Later

Haiku

Greatness is due her
For all the times I cowered
Forgive me, I sinned

I am emotionally constipated.
I take deep breaths to relax
Rest as a laxative
And sometimes, *I laugh*
Big and boisterous

My laugh has been on the spit of many roasting
sessions
Has been the subject of choice words a time or
two

My laugh has gotten me through the most
uncomfortable situations
It has taken me on vacation in the middle of a
nightmare

My laugh does not scare easily
It does not run and hide
Instead, it hydes my skin
So that I may withstand the parasites

Who would attempt to feed off my light until I
had nothing left

My laugh is fresh to death
It has the most exquisite taste in humor
Humbles me when I start taking myself too
seriously

My laugh loves me when the wind gets to
blowing
And the floods get to flowing
And the lightning starts flashing
And the breakers start crashing

My laugh told the storm's legend to Greg
O'Quinn
In a wave of hysteria
Dark comedy is my life's favorite genre of play

My laugh has made a way for me to keep up
the act

My laugh is the greatest comeback story

My laugh can bring you back from the sunken
place

My laugh created open space in my chest
For all the heartbreak to escape
And all the love to survive

My tears confide in *my laugh*

They trust it's stability and ability to keep a
secret

My laugh is at times an honest mistake
I was in my head about something that was
said
Had nothing to do with this conversation

My laugh is often vacant of cause
Pause

When I was in my early twenties, I was
playing video games at my homeboi's house
when he randomly pulled out his penis and
smacked me with it.
I laughed.
Until this day, I cannot tell you why.
Wasn't nuthin' funny. He put it away. I beat
him in the game and went home disgusted with
myself.

Whole & Complete

I'm the mama who tried to warn you there'd be
days like this
The prophetess and the myth
The messenger and the message.

I am a blessing therefore I am blessed
I am what became of my ancestor's reign and
descent
I was never meant to survive it
Nevertheless, here I am thriving.

I am alive and well
I am healing myself
Forgiving missteps

I am drifting a little farther and loving a little
harder
I am safe harbor
For the harbored resentment against the
misfits and outcasts

Cast your cares upon me
Confront me with all of your corrective
suggestions
I am collecting
To hang on the walls of my studio sessions

Each one a lesson on just how mistaken you
must be
To attempt control over Queen

I am the land of the free
On my feet despite my scars
My unbarred bars are unabashed by the brash
things you say

To state trooper my parade
I am still afloat
Although they turn black folks to ghosts every
day
I am unphased by the demons of yesterday

I am today and forever
I am the ever glowing muse of the creator
I am more than skin deep
I've no Emmy
But the world in my hands is no challenge
I am balanced enough to congratulate true
talent
And evaluate the talons of those who pick apart
my gifts

I AM the A list
Authentic
Audacious
Atomic
I'm the bomb diggity erotic
Bionic like Babs
Somewhere in the lab cooking up substance
I am sustenance

Feast your eyes upon me whole
I am the soul outside your window
I am chocolate covered sunshine
I am divine intervention
I am mission accomplished
I am monument to the struggle
Steel spined in my hustle
I am trouble

                    . . .the good kind

I am the unkilled revolution
I am Fred Hampton's dying wish
I am fish in the sea that stands alone amongst
plenty

I am empty of tolerance for fuckery and
bullshit
I am a movement by myself
I am determined to make me better

I am the letter N Nico lent to the Arlington
Expressway
I am Easter Sunday

I am rose and thorn
It's as though I am born with a purpose that's
larger than life

I am fair fight
I am the caged bird's plight

I am a freedom song
Awakening the memories of home

Open Chest

The first time JB punched me in my chest
He knocked the wind from my
adolescent,
    Not yet pubescent, lungs.
        I felt accomplished
        Accepted
            Welcome.

*I'd been begging to play open chest with
the boys for months*
    *They'd always say, "NO. GIRLS.
ALLOWED!"*
    *But then, Daniel said that I didn't count
because I was in the IBTC. The Itty Bitty Titty
Committee.*

It embarrassed me
    I felt ugly
        Rejected
            Unfit

*It was a split decision but I acquired
enough votes to play. Days went by before any
of them caught me with my hands down. I'd
been knocking the dust off them clowns for
hours. But then, behind the fellowship hall
JB stalled me.*

Ebony Payne-English 64

He asked me if I ever kissed anyone before
I said, "No."
He asked if he could kiss me.
I said yes and held my
breath.

He pressed his lips to mine
Then punched me in my chest
So hard that my eyes welled

Even then, I just didn't have it in me to
cry over a boy.
So I took a deep breath and laughed
"You caught me slippin'," I said.
"I know," he said.

We never mentioned it again
Ever since then, I breathe different
I move different
Whenever I am on stage, my first instinct is
stillness
I plant my feet
Raise my head
Open my mouth
I am a powerhouse
Parted lips shout the bellowing echoes of my
soul.

I do not trust the rest of my body with
my honesty.

Only my tongue
    I learned young
        The awkward treachery of
        this temple
            I am still unlearning
            myself

So that I may learn myself better
I was late to my dance lesson today
I'd just left a four-hour play rehearsal
My instructor greeted me with a smile

    I am not in the mood to move.

I am sore
    I am tired
        I am busy

    *I recenter my energy enough to begin
warm up.*

Lesson 1: Stretch

    Instructor: Does it hurt?
    Me: Yes
    Instructor: Good. Keep breathing.

Lesson 2: Do not cut your movements at the wrists.

    *When you commit, do it even with your
fingertips.*

Ebony Payne-English 66

Instructor: Does it feel uncomfortable?
Me: Yes
Instructor: Good. Keep breathing.

Lesson 3: If you know you've made a mistake, keep moving through the motion.

Move on to the next step, don't dwell in imperfection.

Instructor: Do you feel vulnerable?
Me: Yes
Instructor: Good. Keep breathing.

Whenever I encounter trauma,
        the first thing that goes is my breath.
                I'm not quite sure why.

It's as if I can't process oxygen and heartache at the same time

Lesson 4: Breathe through the dance.

Find the places within the piece to catch breath.

Don't hold it in.
        When you breathe deeply,
                It purifies yourself and the audience.

I hear you Dear Hearts
Your part is to remind me to breathe
I never understood the relationship's
mechanics
Until I learned to foster exchange

Lesson 5: New dynamics mean new posture.

I have discovered my fluidity
My house is no longer where my power lies
I have stepped outside
I have extended the appendages of my secret
garden

*It's different when you're fighting for
and with your crowd versus simply
entertaining them.*

Therapeutic Raincoats

Bet you wish you had your raincoat right now
my Dear Sister.

The tropics are roaring
Your fears are exploring the innermost depths
of your livelihood

They think that you should run away
Fade into the night like a disintegrating
nightmare

Fly away from there
Far away from there
Disappear

Because you are barren
You are no longer a contributing member of
society

What good's a wife if she can't break a spell
Cast over her womb?

Ensuring the doom of seeds yet to be planted
That woman's damaged
Find another one
Who can bare a son

Federal decree has been set
I can only imagine the kind of wet it gets
From the acidic rain of the powers that be
And you just want to be free
But there's a bar on your celibacy
And/or your inability to conceive

This is how you measure a woman's worth
Her avoidance of childbirth labels her a
deserter
One abandoning the laws of national continuity
To ensure the perpetuity of the Romanian race

It's a role every girl over 14 years old must take
Or face the consequences
She winces at the thought of the precipitous
poison
That trickles down from Nicolae's compound
To the gutters around the slums
Overrun with new mothers unable to provide
for their young

1 in 10 were born underweight
The unwanted survivors met their fate at the
orphanages
Because the law forbade abortion and did
nothing to promote life

Your untended cries rain cold on your souls
And I know you wish you had your raincoat
So I clothe you in this poem.

Speak your name when I'm alone with my
thoughts
Of worthy causes forgot
Of a dictatorship's acid raindrops
On the tops of the heads of its daughters
Who harbor the sacred secrets of the universe
in their wombs.

Involuntarily turned to assembly lines of mass
production
Her body functions for this purpose
After all, it is her reasonable service to society

Yes, I believe the tears and the sweat
The bloodstains on hospital beds have left her
dripping
Wishing she had shelter or protection
So I speak your contraception
To blockade repeated mistakes
To eliminate political horrors from traveling
time in stealth
Because we all know history repeats itself
Especially when there's no warning on the
bottle of power Kool-Aid
Made from plastic promises
And honest is absent from the label

Unstable motives enable holes in infrastructure
As hymens rupture
Along with marriages disparaged with multiple
miscarriages
Beginning in 1966

Romanian households were taxed an additional
30% of their salaries
If they didn't continuously conceive until May
of 1990

Leaving an unsightly stain on the brain of
Romanian females
Unable to scale heaven's walls
To rise above the rainfall
So I call their experience into remembrance
and light
Basking in the aftermath of their plight
Soaking in hope that floats as we mourn and
cope
Cloaked in therapeutic raincoats

The Butterfly Effect

I long for freedom
The kind that allows you to spew truth at a
moment's notice
And it don't feel like poison
And it don't alienate your lovers
And it don't cause your parents to discover
that their love has limits and conditions.

I need more time
To think
To solution myself stable
To educate myself capable
of carrying this load on my psyche.

I need more time to grow old
To hold my daughter
To forgive her father
to forgive myself for loving him in the first
place

My wound is my mother's neglect
The seven-year-old girl that lives in my chest
Is bleeding to death
I've not maturated enough to be tunicate

My identity is boss lady Black girl
In a world of rich white men

Running shit and making rules
while murdering the sunny places inside of you

My essence is ancestral magic
Artistic excellence
Finding the relevance in the most insignificant
curiosities
like what's the difference between a moth and a
butterfly?

The most easily noticed is the antennae
For me, it's the moth's obsession with light
I've never seen a butterfly barge into my house
at night
to flutter around my lamp

Ain't that what ugly will do to you?
Have you seeking light from anywhere but
inside of you?
Have you surrounding yourself with strangers?

Dragonfruit

It has been said that dragon fruit tastes of
nothing
Despite the hype of its external
It is often found to be internally insipid

Is there anything worse than being cat-fished by
an exotic fruit
You believed would cunnilingus your tastebuds to
life
Only to be surprised by its vapid underwhelmth?

I have a dress that is tapered like a pitaya
I wore it to a masquerade once
Played the social charade I hate
I'm afraid to be an introvert in public
So I smile and converse about subjects I'd rather
not discuss

I've become a cactus fruit
My flowers only bloom at night
When I'm inside my living room
Music and solitude are my chosen photosynthesis

Perhaps you expected more excitement than I
provided
Or was capable of harvesting from my anxiety

Perhaps I never quite satisfied your hunger
For something other than gentle and
understated

Perhaps I am an overrated experience like
dragon fruit

It's more likely that I, too, am a superfood
Consumed for its nutritional gains
As opposed to trivial things such as dramatic
effect
You seem not to recollect
How I never made a request to be picked in the
first place.

For Colorful Girls

No matter how nice a person is to me
It's hard to trust it
When they're not nice to themselves

I used to be there
Needing to be needed is how I depleted my well
of self love

My hugs drew dry and deserted
I grew hollow
My heart fallow until I found the will to till it's
soil

During formative years, I toiled and tussled
With self doubt and insecurity
My mysterious heritage was presented to me as
a slave narrative

I experienced difficulty when building my
identity from obscurity
We speak of our ancestry non-definitively
Question and celebrate the half-baked 28 day
lesson in February

American history has miscarried our tales of
triumph
Aborted our stories of glory

77 Bits & Pieces: After Therapy for Black Women

Poorly parented youth searching for truth

We will never find it at school
But Gwendolyn Brooks taught me
"We Real Cool"

I followed the breadcrumbs to Alex Haley's
roots
Where Carter G. Woodson told me the truth
About who I used to be before the
miseducation via assimilation

Nina and Lauren spoke in a tongue that was
foreign to me
Not the humility disciplined into my dark skin
It was confidence and I dove in
Under their tutelage,
I got me some young, black, and giftedness

I decided to share myself with the world
Poured out my art to the thirstiest of vessels

They swelled, fattened
Some burst with agape favors

From their favorite bleeding heart
I have starved myself to feed someone else
I have Ntozake Shange'd many of my days
Lady in Green gave my stuff away
I've *Lady in Red*ded a strange man in my bed
And cried my exploit into my embroidered
diary
I have *Lady in Blue*d a fetus out of me

*Lady in Yellow*ed into HIV
*Lady in Purple*d my reflection a goddess
Found that *Lady in Orange* in her most forlorn
state

A poet who danced to get rid of the weight
Twerkin' as if her fate depended on it
Dancing keeps us from crying and dying

The *Lady in Brown* keeps reminding me of
Toussaint L'Ouveture's success
But Huey P. Newton at his best found no rest
And can attest
That my revolution may very well be suicide
When the rainbow is not enough to guide me to
the light

I dimmed to make her, him, and them more
comfortable
My humble was once willing to suffer
So that others could be pleased

I evolved to choose me
I learned to eat, sleep, and hydrate
To meditate and take breaks
To vacation and decline calls
To never give my all because when I once had
nothing left,
They all left
And all I had was myself to depend on

I did not let me down
I fixed my crown and drowned in the depths of
my divinity

If a man is to love me, he must first love
himself.
I have not enough nourishment to share my
well or my wealth.

Meditation II: Be Gentle

Dear Mahogany Rose,

Your mother is the most layered sediment
Her hardness has often served as impediment
You made me no longer negligent of my
gentleness

Today is April 11th, 2020
The world is in timeout

We have been quarantined together for a month
now
You are starting to act out
Today alone, you ran into the street;
Tried to climb on the table and hit your head;
Climbed over the couch and almost fell on your
head;

Got into my deodorant;
Got into your baby lotion;
Put multiple inedible objects in your mouth;
Bit me; kicked me; and dropped my computer
on the floor

I sent you to your room and told you to go to bed
You cried
You screamed at the top of your lungs,
"I'm sorry Mommy!"

81 *Bits & Pieces: After Therapy for Black Women*

I deserved the apology and accepted it
You don't have days like this often
Your aunt came to relieve me for a few hours
All I can do with this time is write
About you!

Ebony Payne-English 82

Mattie's Piece

"Da-da" rolls from Mahogany Rose's tongue
with a jolly ease
The same way it did for me 37 years ago
I am waiting to know if she will ever know
That "Mama . . ."
While harder to say, is a gracious call to prayer

Creator
You are are often misgendered in sacred text
books
Successful men have attempted to erase you
the best way they can
With an idea

Destiny would have it not so
They may sleep on your woes
While the whole world rests on your shoulders
But your dreams have awoke the godhood once
spoke of
Better inspired by a mother's love than a baby
daddy's neglect

I regret the day I took off my crown to ground
myself in his arms
Far from exaltations birth-righted to me
I wanted to be more palatable for him to digest
More palpable for his touch

Stardust is cumbersome in the throat
Of those who choke on their own lies

Love has been the demise
Of all who did not first contribute to
themselves

Distance is fonder of smaller hearts than yours
My dearest, endless mother love
What did you keep?
She says, "Only what was necessary."

"What did you leave behind?"
She says, "The dead and the weight."

Family has never escaped your protection
"How do you know them?"
She tells me, "Legacy is always familiar when
you encounter it."

Happiness has evaded many of these exchanges
Pride would cause the menfolk to disagree
Inside of me is a place of empathy
For the silent tears of our *grand* mothers
Every one of them face down in a war room or
prayer closet

This one is for them
A requiem for the OGs
A tribute to the life givers
A poem for the portals
A memorial for the teachers

The sacred waters
The truth tellers
The defenders of all things beautiful
Their womb
Their wind
Their reign

The ancestors came to me on the beach
It was March 13, 2017.

During a thunderstorm
They made jubilee out of forlorn
In honor of the born who give birth
And my dear Mother Earth
And all the hurt in little girls' eyes
Who eye me from the back of a classroom
Who have not yet found the courage
To brave bullies, bad grades, and broken
homes
Without their headphones
So they look on ahead at me from between
their earbuds
Learning the love leaping from my lectures
Is a product of every kind gesture
I've received from a perceived enemy
When I was fighting for my life

This is for my pride
And it taking a hint of when to take several
seats
This is the story of that magic
That some will never appreciate
Although they benefit from it everyday

This is my attempt to pay homage to the color
purple
And the wildflowers

This is for that power the Spice Girls knew
rested within
Even when we are off key, doors are still
opening

The unlocked Pandora's box of the universe
Lurks under skirts between thighs of all sizes
And reserves the right to deny you a peek

This is for those who try to speak nice
To those who despise all languages unamerican

This is for the intelligent
Who are reduced to physical attributes
In boardrooms their work ethic put them into

This is for all the unconquerable women
Whose granny's scrubbed baseboards
In homes they could never afford
Now their grandbabies sit in these boardrooms
In ankara pant suits
Like giants
Defiant and aglow
With their prayers
With their tears
With their legends
Rolling with a grateful ease from our tongues

Bits & Pieces *VI*
PMS

My whole life I tried to be a quality product of my environment, not just another statistic. And yet, here I am.

Not only am I a young, Black woman who has been publicly vocal about having contracted HIV, I am now a baby mama who can't get the assistance she needs voluntarily. So, she is faced with the added humiliation of going before the judge to petition for court-ordered financial input from her co-parent.

I got my period yesterday and it made me tired. It gave me cramps. And perhaps it's just PMS, but being a strong Black woman became a little too much for me to handle today without a good honest cry.

And Lost . . .

We draw our own conclusions in chalk lines
Our kind has always made miraculous martyrs

Their murders make media magic
The most marvelous cold cases

But we dig our own graves don't we?
How dare we be brave or brilliant or Black?

While their widows and children mourn
We march or picket or riot
Or rot away inside
From the helplessness
Or grief or fear or disgust
Or maybe we just post RIP as our status
To be critiqued by the masses

How dare we be late?
Perhaps it would be better if we were never
If a Black body falls from its frame
And there is no hashtag to claim it
Does it make a sound?

When it crashes to the ground
All bloody
All broken
All American casualty

My community is riddled with tragedy
Tangled in the complexity of,
    "We Black out here!"
And . . .
    "We can't just come out and do it any
way we want to!"

Steve Harvey's coon croons a lot like common
sense
Since I've had the time to reflect
My intellect rejects things that don't seem
natural

Meanwhile my body just adapts
Continues to breathe and heartbeat through
the abnormalities

Continues to keep my hands on the steering
wheel
And eyes facing forward

Continues to part it's lips and say, "Yes, Sir."
When asked if knowing how fast I was going
Continues to reach into my wallet
Knowing an unconstitutional ID check is a lot
less inconvenient
Than an untimely death

Will Da Real one was shot in front of his Black
owned business
In his own hometown

Nipsey Hustle was gunned down the same way
No,
It is not Groundhog's Day.
Just April Fools showered with sobs
Gold teethed gods
Immortalized by a brutal blaze of bullets

    "But the one in front of the gun lives
forever."

Excuse me if I don't celebrate
Excuse me if I may weep
If I cannot keep Kendrick's promise to sing

The sting of it all has silenced the melody
This is why we can't have nice things
Like men and victories and pride and dignity

They are taken much easier than they came
We are ashamed to have loved them in the first
place
For allowing our digits
To dig into the caped hem of their garments
And find wholeness and hope

When Tupac died (*was stole),
I cried but did not cope
I was old enough to know what would happen
before it happened
Because this is what happens
Right?!

"If a man has not found something for
which he would die, he isn't fit to live."

This world wants more out of me than I am
willing to give
Similar to all of the men I have loved . . .

                   . . . And lost.

Today

Today, I laughed and giggled with my three
sisters
       I remembered how healing hilarity could
be

Today, I watched my youth write themselves
free
        I remembered how healing honesty
could be

Today, I put on red lipstick and stilettos
       I remembered how healing sexy could
be

Today, I sang, "Get Me Bodied!" at the top of
my lungs in VIP

Today, I remembered me

Today, I remembered how healing I could be
       For myself by myself when necessary

Today, my dreams and aspirations got a little
scary and complex

Today, I was reminded to stretch, flex, and
show myself approved

Today, I remembered you
   The crescent moon beaming above
   your chin as you read this excerpt

Today, I remembered to twerk my soul happy

Today, I was happy to be nappy and southern
and musical and alive

Today, I remembered . . .

we survived!

Meditation III: Be Grateful

Dear Mahogany Rose,

> You are a masterpiece
> You are a master peace
> You are a master piece

> On April 5, 2020 I found a list that I wrote
> when you were in NICU
> It was all of the things I wanted to manifest

> Some of them I can attest were further from
> reach than I imagined
> Some of then have already happened
> Some of them I no longer need
> Thank you for choosing me to be the portal that
> conceived your divine energy
> I love you.

> I have a beautiful view.
> I live near a body of water we have access to
> I am healthy and happy
> I create art that sustains our livelihood
> Makes me feel good
> And helps other people heal

Ebony Payne-English 95

My life is fulfilled and full of purpose
The Random Happenings is illustrated,
complete, and published

I am alive to enjoy the fruits of my labor
We live comfortably with each other
We have more blessings to discover
I'm so grateful to be your mother

Colossus

Spirit is a constant guide
I am a rebellious wanderer
Incredulously following the crimson crumbed
trail of my broken heart

Not all who wander are lost
Not all who follow are sheep
I am learning things now that I knew before I'd
been assimilated
Into the behaviors created by generations of
mistaken identity

My father's native language energetically
dances from my mouth
It is off beat and off key
As I sing the praises of the Asante
It still comes to me

Baba calls it genetic memory
Says the ancestors will always find a way to get to me
Told me storytelling is one of the most potent
forms of alchemy

My tongue is a conflicted weapon awaiting
repurposing
Every poem produces the possibility to wield
my power for good

Ebony Payne-English 97

But good is subjective and relative
What is negative today
May be necessary tomorrow for survival

I am incessantly mindful of the hero's tragic
flaw
To save or be saved is a question that plagues
my action and intent
It is a gift and contradiction

Asking for help is perceived as weakness
And weakness is perceived as blood in the
water
Of the shark tank that harbored my childhood
My youth turned me into the wildest hurricane

The last place I found myself was on my
therapist's couch.

Have you ever been condemned by the wind of
your own tornado?
Been singed by the heat of the fire it started?
Ever been disheartened by words spoken in
affirmation?

Have you ever been taken by a twister?
Blistered by the blaze of your own flames
Spit with intent to heal but instead peeled the
scab from a sore on your soul
So old you were certain it couldn't hurt you
anymore?

Sometimes the stories we tell prove we are not
as well as we thought
It is not lost on me that trauma plants itself
deeply in my pen
It seeps out in every word I scribe or breathe
As release to keep from drowning in depression
Sometimes I get carried away inside my own
whirlwind . . .

Acknowledgements

I deeply desire to give voice and explanation to those feelings buried in the pits of stomachs, plaguing people with the idea that no one else is afflicted in the same way. Loneliness is an illusion and separation is an opportunity to learn something about yourself.

The most lonely and separated period of my life came by way of becoming a single mother. I was not ready for all that I would feel.

The first two years of my daughter's life were some of the lowest emotional experiences I've ever encountered; balanced with the deepest love I've ever known. A love that I imagine could only exist between a mother and their child.

What was most interesting about my mental struggles during this time was the fact that I'd been around many single mothers throughout my journey. They told me about the financial burdens, the tough conversations, and the awkward moments when engaging with their baby daddy's family. The one thing none of those women ever expressed to me was how painful it is to be abandoned by the father of your child.

I thought something was wrong with me because I was having such a hard time coping. I thought maybe I was incompetent or not as magical as the other women in my family who experienced the same things I had with a smile on their faces and joy in their hearts.

Due to my previous history of depression and self-harm, I did the most responsible thing I could think of to do for myself. I got a therapist and then sought out a priestess in hopes of recentering myself with peace, joy, and acceptance.

There is a place inside of me that harnesses inexhaustible energy to speak what I speak and write what I write while reaching toward the sky. *After Therapy* is a collection of poems that I am able to share with the world as my proclamation that I am enough for me.

Through the love of myself, I am able to release all who cannot love me in a way that encourages and affirms my highest self. I am able to accept love in various forms instead of concentrating on the ways in which I've been disappointed.

After Therapy is a note to self that today is enough for me. For if I master today, tomorrow is a continuation of yesterday's greatness.

When I decided to publish this book, I reached out to the women in my tribe to assist and ensure I didn't chicken out. Some elders, some friends, some teachers. I am grateful to Nikesha Elise Williams for finding this work worthy to publish. I am blessed by Yvette Angelique Hyater-Adams who thought this work worthy to edit. I am honored by Nicole "Nico" Holderbaum who believed this work worthy of her cover design. To all of the women in my village that never let me drown, I love you to life. May your hearts be light as a feather.

Asé

About the Author

Ebony Payne-English is an author, performer, playwright, and educator from Duval County, Florida. She is the first woman to establish her own chapter of the international poetry organization, Black on Black Rhyme.

The author of graphic novel, *The Random Happenings*, as well as award winning poetry collection, *Secrets of Ma'at*, Ebony's discography includes 7 albums: *Old Soul* (2006), *Struggle's Embrace* (2010), *EbEnFlo* (2012), *School Beats* (2013), *Know Love* (2015), *Kuongoza* (2021), and *Bits & Pieces (2022)*.

Her first short film titled after her 6th studio album, *Kuongoza*, is the winner of Best Artistic Film at the 2021 Detroit Black Film Festival.

She currently serves as Executive Director of The Performers Academy, a 501c3 arts education organization and is a founding member of the Board of Directors for Southern Fried Poetry, Inc. which produces the largest adult regional poetry slam in the nation.

CPSIA information can be obtained
at www.ICGtesting.com
Printed in the USA
LVHW111616060722
722787LV00002B/6